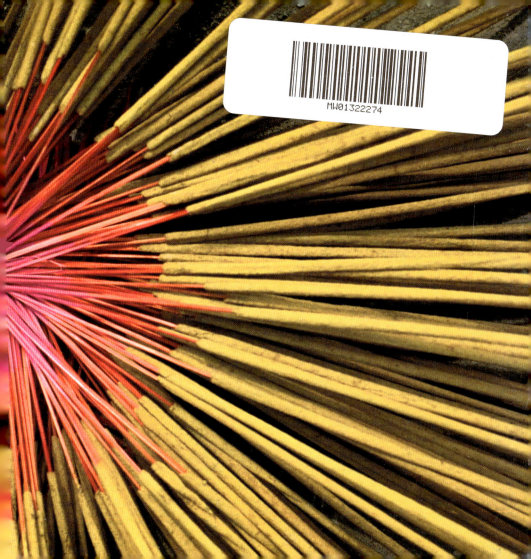

soul - noun

The spiritual or immaterial part of a human being
or animal, regarded as immortal.

A person's moral or emotional nature or sense of identity.

The essence of something.

Emotional or intellectual energy or intensity,
esp. as revealed in a work of art or an artistic performance.

A person regarded as the embodiment of a specified quality.

An individual person.

A person regarded with affection: a nice old soul.

Synonyms: spirit, essence, self, inner being, life force, individuality.

Get better please ...

SOUL

Heart, mind, body, spirit.

Designed by Suzanne and Barbara Maher

PUBLISHING HOUSE

living words

First published in 2009
Copyright © Affirmations Publishing House 2009

All rights reserved.

Published by
Affirmations Publishing House
34 Hyde Street, Bellingen NSW 2454 Australia
t: +61 2 6655 2350
e: sales@affirmations.com.au
www.affirmations.com.au

Designed and Edited by
Suzanne and Barbara Maher
Images © Lonely Planet Images

ISBN 978-0-9805377-3-4

10 9 8 7 6 5 4 3

While every effort has been made to acknowledge the author of the quotations used,
please notify the publisher if this has not occurred.

Printed in China on recycled paper using vegetable based inks.

Affirmations are living words that bring meaning to life,
giving memories to share with everyone, everywhere.

Sounds you can see,
Colours you can feel,
Light you can hear.

Namaste

As a single footstep
will not make a path on the earth,
so a single thought will not
make a pathway in the mind.
To make a deep physical path,
we walk again and again.
To make a deep mental path,
we must think over and over
the kind of thoughts we wish
to dominate our lives.

HENRY DAVID THOREAU

Why take
when you could be giving.
Why watch
as the world goes by.
It's a hard enough life to be living,
why walk
when you can fly.

People who are crazy enough
to think that they can change the world
are the ones that usually do.

Let your soul
radiate peace.
Think, act and
speak harmoniously.
Be contented
and thankful for
all that you have.
Live your life
as a divine vision.

HAZRAT INAYAT KHAN

If the only prayer
you said in your whole life
was "thank you",
that would suffice.

MEISTER ECKHART

For one human being
to love another:
that is perhaps
the most difficult
of all our tasks,
the ultimate, the
last test and proof,
the work for which
all other work
is but preparation.

RAINER MARIA RILKE

Ask,
and the answer
shall be given.

RUMI

One drop of water
helps to swell the ocean;
a spark of fire
helps to give light to the world.
None are too small
to be of service.
Think of this and act.

The thought
manifests as the word,
the word manifests as the deed,
the deed develops into habit,
and habit hardens into character.
So watch the thought
and its way with care
and let it spring from love.

BUDDHA

We do not see things as they are. We see them as we are.

THE TALMUD

Be rich in admiration
and free from envy,
rejoice in the good of others,
love with such generosity of heart
that your love is still a dear possession
in absence or unkindness:
these are true gifts.

ROBERT LOUIS STEVENSON

Occasionally
what you have to do
is to go back to the beginning
and see everything
in a new way.

PETER STRAUB

The advantage of being tiny:
Like a blade of grass looking up at a tree,
Like a stream looking out on the ocean,
Like a light in a village hut
looking up at the stars in the sky;
Because being tiny
you can see what is great.

The only lifelong, reliable motivations
are those that come from within,
and one of the strongest of those
is the joy and pride
that grow from knowing
that you've just done something
as well as you can do it.

LLOYD DOBENS

Teachers
open the door,
but you must enter
by yourself.

CHINESE PROVERB

If you are pained
by external things,
it is not they
that disturb you,
but your own judgment of them.
And it is in your power
to wipe out that judgment now.

MARCUS AURELIUS

A positive attitude
causes a chain reaction
of positive thoughts,
events and outcomes.
It is a spark
that creates extraordinary results.

Try to be better than yourself.

WILLIAM FAULKNER

Life is to be measured
not so much by the position you reach,
as by the obstacles that you overcome
while trying to succeed.

BROOKER T WASHINGTON

We determine
our destination,
what kind of road
we will take to get there,
and how happy we are
when we arrive.

The spirit within you
is a river.
Its sacred bathing place
is contemplation;
Its waters are truth;
Its banks are holiness;
Its waves are love.

HITOPADESA

The essential sadness
is to go through life without loving.

But it would be almost
equally sad to leave this world
without ever telling those you loved
that you love them.

Gratitude is the best attitude.

Everyone has inside of them
a piece of good news.
The good news is
that you don't know how great you can be,
how much you can love,
what you can accomplish,
and what your potential is.

Our lives
are not determined
by what happens to us,
but by how we react
to what happens.

Not by
what life brings to us,
but by the attitude
we bring to life.

Now. This is it.
The whole purpose and meaning
for the existence of everything.

Enjoy the little things,
for one day you may look back and realise
they were the big things.

All the peace, wisdom
and joy in the universe
are already within us;
we don't have to gain,
develop or attain them.

We merely need to open our eyes
and realise what is already here,
and who we really are.

When a great moment
knocks on the door of your life,
very often it's no louder
than the beating
of your heart.

BORIS PASTERNAK

The only person
you are destined to become,
is the person
you decide to be.

RALPH WALDO EMERSON

A positive attitude
really can
make dreams come true.

If you know
what you want out of life,
it's amazing how opportunities
will come to enable you
to carry them out.

JOHN M GODDARD

Change is not something that we should fear.
Rather, it is something that we should welcome.
For without change,
nothing in this world
would ever grow or blossom,
and no one in this world
would ever move forward
to become the person they're meant to be.

Praise and blame,
gain and loss,
pleasure and sorrow
come and go like the wind.
To be happy, rest like a giant tree,
in the midst of them all.

BUDDHA

Greet everyone you meet with a warm smile.
No matter how busy you are,
don't rush encounters with
co-workers, family and friends.
Speak softly. Listen attentively.
Act as if every conversation you have
is the most important thing on your mind today.
Look your children and your partner
in the eyes when they talk to you.
Stroke the cat, caress the dog.
Lavish love on every living being you meet.
See how different you feel at the end of the day.

SARAH BAN BREATHNACH

Listen to your intuition,
it will tell you
everything
you need to know.

Our deepest fear
is not that we are inadequate.
Our deepest fear
is that we are powerful beyond measure.
It is our light, not our darkness,
that most frightens us.

We ask ourselves,
"Who am I to be brilliant,
gorgeous, talented and fabulous?"
Actually, who are you not to be?

You are a child of God;
your playing small
doesn't serve the world.

MARIANNE WILLIAMSON

Miracles
surround us on every hand.
Life itself
is the miracle of miracles.

GEORGE BERNARD SHAW

Success lies just beyond your thoughts.

Know this understanding
is what inspires you to accomplish
what you really desire in life.

If you are satisfied with yourself
and your thoughts,
there is nothing you cannot do or be.

Your thoughts are powerful.

Be true
to your work,
your word,
and your friend.

HENRY DAVID THOREAU

Always do
what you are
afraid to do.

RALPH WALDO EMERSON

The first step
toward getting somewhere
is to decide that you are
not going to stay
where you are.

CHAUNCEY DEPEW

It is not length of life,
but depth of life.

RALPH WALDO EMERSON

Be sure to cultivate positive thinking
for the right reasons -
to enhance the quality of your life
and the lives of others.

Honour and cherish the light and love
that emanates from within.

Since everything in life
is but an experience,
perfect in being what it is,
having nothing to do with good or bad,
acceptance or rejection,
one may well burst out in laughter.

LONG CHEN PA

The mind becomes clear and serene
when the qualities of the heart are cultivated.

Friendliness toward the joyful,
compassion toward the suffering
and happiness toward the pure.

Listen to your heart,
for it knows the truth.

Life is a path.
If you follow your heart
it will lead you in the right direction.

Take every opportunity
that is offered in your life.

The pattern of our thoughts
creates our karma,
which develops in this sequence:

A thought or idea is followed by an action;
from an action comes a habit;
from habit comes a character;
and from a character
comes a destiny.

Affirmations Publishing House

Creators of gift books, greeting cards and paper products.

To view the range of products, visit our website

www.affirmations.com.au